WHEN YOU SAVE YOURSELF

i dedicate this book to my *mother*

the one who saved herself by becoming exactly the woman she dreamed of being when she was younger, and the woman she needed, but never had growing up

she became the hero of her story,
and taught me to become the hero of mine

after all these years
i have realized
no one ever loved me more
than my mother

self

what an illusion
thinking a man
would save me
only to find out
i was the hero
of my own story
all this time

it is important to be there for yourself
and to love her fully
so even if they abandon you
you still have your back
and you still find a way
to exist wholly
with or without
the presence
of somebody else

i have said 'i love you' so many times
to others
and it felt completely natural,
but when i tried to say it to myself
suddenly, the feeling was foreign
that's when i realized
i had overlooked
the one that needed my love
the most
self

true self connection
happens when you manage
to be in peace and silence within
even when the outside world
is loud and chaotic

spend some time alone,
you will realize a lot

when was the last time
you did something
just for yourself?

how empowering to know
i will always have myself
even if everyone
turns their backs
on me

maybe what you need
is simply a break
and to take some time
to rest

no one can take better care of you,
than you

don't be so quick
to blame yourself
for everything,
sometimes we are
are own harshest critics

did you know
your inner self speaks to you?
it happens when you stay in silence
undisturbed by the voices
and opinions of others.
when you listen to your heart
all the noise outside stops

you look happier
since you put yourself first
without accommodating
the needs of everyone else
before yours

growth

hard times
hurt me
but they also shaped me
into who i am today

i love seeing glimpses
of the child within me
showing up time after time
there's still a little girl inside
living under the layers
of an adult
who tries so hard to be responsible
and in control of life
and who often takes herself
too seriously,
aching to be free

knowing your worth
doesn't mean you become
selfish or distant to people
you were once close with,
it means you carefully choose
to give your time and energy
to those who can see
the value and the beauty in you

throughout the years
i've known different versions of myself
so i am enjoying the present moment,
the way i am
until it's time
to change again

- *growth*

the change will happen
when you become too big
for your current situation

- *outgrowing your environment*

i no longer
seek validation
in people
i wouldn't even go to
for advice

at the end of the day
no one can save you,
but you

how beautiful to change
and turn into the person
you always wanted to be,
but in order to grow
and transform
you have to let go
of the person you were
before

i learned to be happy,
but not satisfied.
i became grateful for what i had,
yet eager to reach bigger goals
so i could keep growing

maybe if we focused more
on bettering ourselves
instead of trying to find
all the wrongdoings in others
we would be able to build
stronger relationships

the younger me
would be in awe
if i told her
the things we did
and the dreams
we built
in our reality

don't forget to
look back now and then
just to see how far you have come;
sometimes we need to remind ourselves
where we started
and how far we have arrived

loneliness

i sometimes wonder
what it could have been

i would accept a hurtful ending
for as long as
the story we wrote
was unforgettable

i wish you could take my eyes
and see yourself
the way i see you

people won't always believe
in your dreams
or what you say
you will achieve
so you have to be unwavering
in your conviction
that you can,
and you will

do you ever feel
like you are in the wrong place?

i know loneliness is hurtful
yet, strangely more bearable
than staying in the company
of the wrong people

maybe i hadn't fully known you
or maybe you grew away from me
until i realized
we were worlds apart

sometimes all you have left
is you

loneliness never scared me
i found in myself
a fulfilling company

it is a wakeup call
once you realize
nobody is coming to save you,
but you

it is in the moments
i feel the loneliest,
i listen to myself
the most clearly

freeing yourself

maybe i can't be completely free
until i choose myself
unconditionally

what a great relief
to stop worrying about
how others perceive you
and begin to act
the way you want to see yourself
becoming

that deep desire you feel
when you want more,
when you crave more
is your *potential*
to have more,
and be more

it is often only after you leave a toxic environment,
you realize you were in one

sometimes, you don't have to push yourself harder,
sometimes, all you need is to give yourself permission
to rest

my need to protect my peace
is stronger than my need
to prove you wrong
- *arguing*

doing something i don't want
to please others
feels like a betrayal to myself
like i am at war
with an enemy
that should have always
been my ally

sometimes overthinking
makes things look worse
than they really are

- get out of your head

maybe you didn't achieve your dreams today,
maybe it was one of those days when
your greatest achievement
is making it through
and that is good enough

i stopped taking my past hurt
into new beginnings

i have come to a time in my life
where i don’t care
if i am included or not

strange looking back
at my past self
knowing i would have done
anything for you
even if it meant
going against myself
only to realize one day
it would have never been enough.
when someone is used to you
choosing them over yourself
they don't consider it a privilege anymore
but start to demand it
and suddenly
you risk losing yourself
in trying to please them

sometimes trying too hard
is not the solution
sometimes letting go
opens the way
for the opportunity
you have been waiting for

love yourself enough to know
when you deserve better

i wonder how many battles
you fought
in silence

sometimes we give up
when success is just
one step ahead
of us

i didn't want to wait
and hope for the best
i demanded of myself
to do everything in my power
to reach the goals
my heart was so earnestly set on

what a never-ending battle it is
fighting to reach your dreams
like you are swimming in a river
against its stream

you should get to that point where
your trust in yourself is stronger
than your doubts and fears
so strong
it mutes all limiting beliefs

sometimes it gets worse
before it gets better
like life is testing you
and rewarding those
who were strong enough
to keep going beyond
the breaking point
of giving up

you can start changing your life, or not
you can start improving yourself, or not
you can start making a difference, or not
it's really up to you
but whatever you do,
know that you have a choice

if today was hard
and you made it through,
it was a good day
and it was enough
even if it was all
you could do

i learned that sometimes fear
doesn't go away until after
you have done the thing
sometimes we have to do it scared
in order to gain the confidence

how freeing
to love yourself first
without waiting for that love
to be given to you
from the outside

fearless

maybe the best way
to overcome fear
is to get face to face
with it

my doubts and fear
started to disappear
once i got to know
myself better
and found out
how strong i could be
when i needed to

how courageous
to be completely
yourself
even when you risk
being different

don't deprive yourself
of dreaming big,
so big your heart
jumps from excitement
every time you think about it

in retrospect
what wasn't meant for me
either left me or never came
despite my best efforts
and although at the time
it felt like the universe
was conspiring against me,
now i know it had planned
bigger and better things
i just had to trust its timing

i have lost in life
but i only considered myself a loser
when i didn't even try
or gave up
ahead of time

maybe your criticism
isn't a form of love,
or encouragement
to become better
but a way to break me
and bring me down
to your level of insecurity

i have found that
people who have
something bad to say
about everyone
don't have a problem
with the whole world,
but with themselves

that moment when you realize
you are surrounded by toxic people
who hurt your mental health
and you finally have the strength
to move away from them

i'm sorry i can't fit into
the image you have for me,
your fantasy of who i should be
- *i am too busy building the woman*
of my dreams

maybe the failure
was a sign of the progress,
of going in directions
i hadn't been before,
walking into the unknown,
of trying new things
and giving myself a chance
to reach new destinations

how beautiful
to fail,
and then learn,
and then fix,
and then overcome,
and then one day
to finally succeed
after all the struggle,
and hardships,
and setbacks

no matter what is being said
against loneliness
i have learned it is better to be alone
than surrounded by the wrong people

i am no longer
spending time and energy
in anything
that doesn't fully
interest and excite me

hero

i decided to be
the hero of my own story

the hardest type of confidence to master
is the confidence to be your true self
at all times

how powerful to rely on yourself
knowing whatever happens
you will always find a way
to make it through

all that time wasted
worrying about
what others would think of me
when i could've enjoyed everything
so fully

don’t let anyone convince you
to settle for less than what you want
making you think your dreams are too big for you

what you think is the limit
only shows *your* limit,
i am free to aim
much higher

maybe there is no need
to find out who you really are,
but instead think about
who you want to be,
and then create from scratch
the best version
you can think of yourself

sometimes what others don't like in you
is also what they don't like in themselves

after all this time
i have realized
no one knew
what was better for me
than me

you should BE a priority,
you shouldn't have to convince him
to make you his priority

i often mistook other's limiting beliefs
as my own capability
in what i could, and couldn't do

at the end of the day
no one can save you
but you

beginnings

some endings open the way
for new beginnings

starting over
is hard,
but it's never
too late

one thing i learned in life:
the best is yet to come!
don't stay in a situation
that doesn't serve you anymore
just because you think
it's the best you've ever had.
that doesn't mean
it's as good as it can get

i worked so hard
to make people believe in me
if only i worked as hard
to lose all my doubts and fear
so i could be filled with confidence

i am no longer waiting
for someone to complete me
i am already whole

what a beautiful human being
you find out you are
once you start to
understand yourself

and even when something becomes a memory
it is still part of your story

strange how
when you are broken
even pulling all the pieces together
won't make you go back
to your older version

- some scars remain

when i can't help myself
maybe helping another
will heal me, too

i hate waiting for something i really want
if my heart wants it,
it wants it here,
it wants it *now*

every time i failed
i noticed something in me changed
after every failure there were
lessons learned along the way
they made me a bit wiser, and less scared
to try again
and give myself yet another chance
in reaching the destinations
i longed to be

change doesn't start with action
but with one decision.
it's that decision
that pushes your body
to act

resilience

i find comfort in knowing
no matter what obstacles
come my way
i can overcome them

independence to me means
depending on no one
but yourself

when you have nothing to be grateful for
remember to have a look at the sun
that kisses your head with its warmth
remember you woke up today
and each morning gives you another chance
look at the world that moves so fast
and let a smile hug your face
remember all the beautiful things you are able to see
and the breathtaking lines you can read
how lucky we are to be,
how lucky to exist

when i doubt myself
the idea of how proud
that little girl would be
reassures me
that in the end
i am going to be okay

i wish to wake up one day
and know that i am living
exactly the life i chose to live
the kind of life that makes me feel alive,
the kind of life i carefully drew in my mind,
i want to be able to live the way
i always wanted to

'no one is coming to save you'
is not a sad, hopeless truth,
but rather a reinstatement
that you are the hero of your own story

i decided i'd rather
make my own mistakes
and pay the price,
than falter because i listened
to the advice of others
and then resent them
for guiding me
in the wrong direction

sometimes being too independent
happens because you've had
to rely on yourself for so long,
that is the only way you know
how to live

it is never too late
to come back to yourself

no one has ever had
the same life journey as you
therefore, you are writing a story
that has never been written before
make sure to make it one to remember

there is always a chance for you
to reinvent yourself

staying in the comfort zone
for a long time
is more hurtful and damaging
than failing while trying to give your life
a chance to be better

truth

sometimes you already know the answer,
you are just not ready to accept it yet

hard pill to swallow:
sometimes, hard work
doesn’t translate to success

the sad news is
you can be the kindest person
and still be treated badly

i hope one day
you will be happy
not content with what you have,
not hoping it will get better,
not waiting for things to change,
not wishing,
not praying,
not longing
just genuinely,
completely
happy

i have noticed,
those who hurt others,
are hurting inside.
happy people
never find joy
in the suffering of another
misery loves company

maybe i should have listened
to that voice deep down within,
it seems like it knew the truth
from the beginning
- *gut feeling*

i want to make up for the time lost
in not doing what my heart really wanted

what a waste of time
trying so hard
to prove yourself to others
and crave their validation
when you should already know
how worthy you are

to heal,
you have to go through the pain,
you have to face it
in order to overcome it

i felt so relieved
once i realized
perfection can't be reached
because it doesn't exist,
and even if i don't manage to do
everything i have in mind,
doing as much as i can
will always be good enough
i won't push myself so hard
i burn out,
but i will make sure
to make myself proud

when you are stuck
living a life
that is so different
from the one you dream
and want for yourself
it feels like you are underwater
drowning
trying so desperately
to reach the surface
and finally breathe

one of the most important lessons
i learned as a woman
was to never let my self-worth
depend on male validation

i sometimes mute my logic
to let my heart speak
and to be able to hear it
without judgment

longing

sometimes i think about
all the words i needed to say
that never left my lips

maybe it is not the world
that makes you so angry
all the time,
but the dissatisfaction
with yourself
and your life
and the suppressed desires
longing to be fulfilled

perhaps i was meant to live
in another lifetime
one that has already passed
or is still to come

every time i feel alone
i remind myself many people
are feeling the same
i find comfort in knowing
we are feeling lonely together

i have learned that
sometimes
hard work
doesn't translate to success
sometimes you work harder than anyone,
try your best,
give everything you've got,
and still fail
i guess it's part of life

i wonder when does someone stop hoping?
what would be the breaking point?

i always look for
something beautiful
in everyone
and i always find it

i want to grow and transform
so fiercely and completely
into the best version of myself,
i completely die to my past self

i love being lost
in beautiful visions
of a life
i am about to create
what is yours will find its way towards you

what you think is your limit
remains your limit
until you reach it,
then you realize
you could do even more,
strive even higher.
there is so much potential in you
patiently waiting to be used

i sometimes wonder
if it is ever possible
for your reality
to be as beautiful
as your dreams

i didn't lose my older self
i embraced it, and then
when the time was right
i let it go
in order to allow myself
to grow and transform
into a better version

relationships

with or without you
i am at this moment
as complete
as i could ever be

once you realize
no one is coming
to save you
you start to become
the hero of your own story

don't change yourself
to maintain a relationship,
especially if the change
is one-sided

what a heavy feeling
being so disappointed
by someone you trusted
fully

maybe, when someone tries to put you down,
belittle or undermine your confidence
you shouldn't try to prove your worth
or prove them wrong
you just have to walk away
and distance yourself from those
who make you feel small

i never regretted the things
i chose to do on my own
even when i failed
i only regretted the things
i did because i listened to
the opinions of others
or their expectations of me
even when i was going
against myself
and against what deep down
i knew was right

sometimes, you feel more lonely
when surrounded by the wrong people
than when you are alone

the tears i hate the most
are not those of sadness,
but of anger
when you feel like the world
has let you down

i am no stranger
in doing my best
to please others
even when it means
going against
what i want

and then it dawned upon me
that people who are used
to treating you badly
will suddenly get mad
and make you feel guilty
for putting boundaries
like you violated their right
to abuse you

i wonder how many men
look at their wives
like their property
and how many women
allow themselves
to be treated like one

i understood the importance
of surrounding yourself
with the right people
once i spent time with those
who left me feeling good
after i exited the room
instead of misplaced
and exhausted
like i was used to

growing wings

how beautiful to fail,
and learn,
and grow,
and then try again
until you finally make it
knowing you never gave up
on yourself and your dreams

transform that trembling voice inside
that is full of self-doubt
into a confident, loud sound
that is not scared of the world
anymore

you don't have to prove
you are worthy
to anyone
but yourself

what strength and bravery it takes
to fight a battle in silence
i am proud of you

you shouldn't see as competition
the people who have already arrived
where you want to be
they have paved the way for you
and are the living proof
that it can be done
if they did it, you can do it too

i watched a beautiful tree
slowly dry out
and lose its charm
by the harsh conditions
of life;
until one spring day
the sun started shining
replacing the cold
with its warmth
kissing the tree until it started
to slowly bloom again
regaining its vibrant colors,
just like it was before.
i learned from the nature itself
you can fall and raise again
and life goes on,
and there is hope,
and it is not over
until you say so

i started to write about the things
i am most grateful for
every night before i slept
and i noticed so many
wonderful aspects of my life
i had taken for granted

i thought the challenges i faced
along the way
made me stronger,
but now i realize
strength has always been a part of me
maybe dormant, or hidden deep within,
but every time i needed to be strong
there was no need to search for it.
i didn't need to ask for strength
when strong was what
i have always been

every time you face a problem
tell yourself to *rise above it*

just because someone doesn't understand you
the way you had hoped to be understood
doesn't mean you are in the wrong
they are just not able to see what you see,
the same way you see it
and even though you can't find in them
the support you wished you were given
there are always people
who can make you feel validated
and someday you will find them

love

i want someone
that will love me so hard,
it takes away all my insecurities

you never fully realize and cherish
the importance of a moment
until it slips by
and so suddenly
becomes a memory

i am grateful to my mother
for she wanted me to be a full person,
someone who knows she is enough
who knows who she is
and who she wants to become
and has the power and courage
to become it
even if i had to do it alone;
my mother knew what it meant
to be the hero of her own story
and save herself
so she made sure
to guide me
and show me the way

you have to love yourself
in order to be able to love others

if giving our time to others
is considered love
why would giving time
to ourselves
ever be selfish?

often, people who look
too serious and cold
have the softest souls

i realized i had a healthy relationship with myself
when i was comfortable being alone with my thoughts
and i enjoyed my own company just as much
as i enjoyed the company of the people i love the most

i feel like time is
the most precious thing i've got
and we can never know
when it will run out,
so i will make sure to use it
to better myself and feed my soul
and never spend it
on self-sabotaging thoughts

nothing hurts my heart more
than the sound of someone's voice breaking
after trying so hard to hold back their tears

maybe it didn't work
because you deserved better

at the end of my time
i want my mind to overflow
with the memories of a life
well-lived

Made in the USA
Columbia, SC
05 November 2024

0f79531c-6337-41b3-85c6-141573eb95edR01